# SOLE

# IMPRESSIONS

## BARRY STERNLIEB

CODHILL
PRESS

**ALSO BY BARRY STERNLIEB**

*Winter Crows* (Codhill Press)

*Thinning the Rows* (Brooding Heron Press)

*Thoreau's Hat* (Brooding Heron Press)

*Fission* (Adastra Press)

# SOLE
# IMPRESSION

## BARRY STERNLIEB

*Barry Sternlieb*

C

CODHILL PRESS
NEW YORK • NEW PALTZ

CODHILL
**PRESS**

Codhill books are published by
David Appelbaum for Codhill Press

codhill.com

Published in the United States of America

ISBN 978-1-949933-12-3

Cover and Book Design by Jana Potashnik
BAIRDesign, Inc.  · bairdesign.com

FOR MY WIFE AND DAUGHTERS,
AND FOR MY FRIENDS

# CONTENTS

# QUILT

Here is a geography
with no place
for distance, a love

that seams complete
in the scheme of purpose,
a declaration

of dependence between
mother and daughter,
dyed in the wool

spun from birth,
a secret belonging
to wholeness

whose order joins
each pattern
through the intricate

piecework of needle
and thread, a quiet grit
of resistance

passed down by design
to save the world
inside it.

# DRY BRUSH PAINTING
# OF WINTER CROWS

Fed by hunger,
greatness comes down
to a few sudden strokes
of the brush.

In no time, five birds
crack the frozen sky,
vagrant notes
on a scale of space.

At eighty, doing
justice to the way
nature works,
he works like nature,

without a doubt,
holding the line
against illusion
so black and white

ring true as always.
Too simple for words
this flock of crows
gusting past.

Chinese ink, rice paper:
such a small painting
practically empty,
that makes what waits

in the wings
somehow soar
toward the unseen peaks
of our lives.

# SOLE IMPRESSION

No matter how far over the hill
we get, this workhorse press
and I are still on the same page,
throwbacks lying low, bound
by the cause of words.
In the basement shop,
where centuries become hours,
to ink the plate, crank the lever,
then handfeed sheet after sheet
while rollers rasp across type
lays down a beat I can grasp
as if lastingness flows
like current through muscle
and metal, each clearly
moved by the other. Here,
like gnostic gospel, solitude
stacks up against talk,
tapping a cast-iron vein
of tradition whose bottom line
is the obsolete, what doesn't
change, changing hands.
Behind the scenes, priorities
hinge on problems solved
with pure tinkery luck, with
a bond between machines,
one living, one not, but
when bed and platen meet,
when I see the sole
impression of every letter
catching light, it all seems
somehow human, especially
at the end, collating done,

signatures sewn, as we go our
separate ways: this press and I
toward yesterday, to start again
from scratch, the handmade book
toward tomorrow, a newborn
relic, grandfathered in.

# CORCOMROE ABBEY

Finding yourself
in ruins like this
gives neglect another purpose.

Walls sprout flowers
and sky wanders through.
Here, salvation calls

for a Celtic cross
against barren hills,
claiming what remains

to be seen. Those monks
who carved each day
into the afterlife,

whose souls were one
with mallet and chisel,
knew how to make silence

last, their hearts set
on the order
of stone. Even now,

with summer wind
saying mass to perfection,
beauty builds

as it crumbles,
and toward that end
you catch the drift

of permanence
suddenly moving
up the past.

# TEA MASTER
## (16TH CENTURY JAPAN)

Even light, in humility, bows
to reach his garden through maple,
cherry and fern. Clay-fed channels
among islands of flagstone
embroider the ritual path
that his son has twice swept clean today
so each dead leaf set upon it
dignifies the plan.
At a granite, moss-lined well
whose water echoes dark ballets of green,
the guests calmly kneel and wash
desire from their thoughts,
then enter the teahouse
where charcoal evolves into ash
below the master's iron urn.
All minds now root in their awareness,
flourish and bear seed
like the ripped eyelids of the tea father,
Bodhidharma, who found sleep a threat
to his nine-year devotion
watching one stone wall refine him
toward Buddha. Each lid awakened,
an inexhaustible plant, whose power
steeped in peace
can be drawn from this porcelain bowl
then passed around a circle
until beauty greets the master
with need for use.
Order is accomplished.
And hours later, the ceremony done,
he sits alone contemplating silence
in the satisfied garden of himself.

# GODOT IN SARAJEVO, 1993

*for Susan Sontag*

Like a gardener turning to details
of sun and soil, she describes
the continuum of rhythm
even chaos must confide in.

Staging this play where loss
makes the present look old
cedes a common routine
back to second nature.

While the audience tends
a fragile truce of candlelight
and watches the master tramps,
one Muslim, one Serb, face their fears,

life takes after the days
when walking home,
setting a table, and eating a meal
was the natural order

borne out by choice.
How gracefully she downplays
her own close calls
like a chorus keeping the faith

of that makeshift theater
and those inside who find hope
in its hopeless words
completely worth the risk.

# PRINTING BY HAND

It's hard to believe
how small beauty, almost hidden,
can roll through the press
like a summer storm.
I envision wind hounding cinders
of crows from the trees
and rootbound odors citing rain.
Flawless paper is kissed by your lines
on what's taken for granted
right down to the dirty work
no one would choose.
Where lead has a will, ink has a way
and cranking the miles out,
sheet by sheet, rhythm
gathers until it feels
older than faith, wholly untaught,
a point in the test of metal.
A midwife would understand
such finesse of pulse and pressure
when life itself is at stake.
Printing by hand, I can only speak
for a few simple things,
loving how cool cast iron
and reliable words
give none the place of honor,
but all the honor of place.

# MIGRATIONS

Routes take shape
    as flight takes root,
        and lines of geese,
miming tide, look

more like unbound
    scripture, the past
        that comes to pass.
With clocks turned

back, sky spells out
    abandonment in
        the hand of wind,
a pact between cells

when cold lays
    down the law
        and waves of wings
break on time,

inherent faith,
    no different than
        ours, leaving home
to find the way home.

# CALLIGRAPHY

Hoping that characters hold true,
for the final class
the master assigns just two words:
war and peace.

In light of tradition,
he examines every stroke,
satisfied our work on war
has nowhere else to turn,

but peace is another story,
looking too much like language
until the Vietnam vet,
a quiet mechanic

who still walks point
through the jungle of sleep,
leads the group outside
with his word on a rice paper kite

and lets December wind carry it
across the empty sky.

# THE RETURN

Imagine the shock
of a twelve-year-old boy
who goes downstairs one night
to ask the maid a question
and finds her standing at the sink
of her small bathroom,
the door open just enough
for him to see how
she watches herself in the mirror,
gently washing her breasts
with a soft white cloth.
Sparked by darkness,
his eyes comb her body,
but he is still too young
to envision the site,
salty and warm,
where he would take
the cloth from her hand
and hold it under the water
slowing things down
so now and then, a lifetime later,
he could return
to the wetness of that skin,
the smell of that hair like the inlet,
the way she looked
as he washed her.

# BURNING IN SPANISH

To reach the masses
you live with your animals
in the hills,
wanting peace to feel
like a late explosion
of goldenrod around the cabin
or that sharp backlash
of blue after a storm.
On the cracked butcher block
a simple meal waits:
salad, cheese, and the black bread
straight from your mother's memory
which today is just
a crumbling road
through Pittsfield in the sixties,
the same road you followed
to Honduras and Guatemala
whose desperate blessings
nourished you as no god
ever could.
Now, back for good,
with another plan
after all you've done,
you keep to yourself
those lands still burning in Spanish
where you never eat or sleep,
never stop driving
the message home.

# HONORING THE DUST

Barbarians swarmed her borders,
but the arms of Han China
hung still. Lady Ch'eng
was readied for burial:
oiled, hairpiece combed,
flanked by dragons of silk.

The emperor's consort
as China crystallized
a Buddhist age, she bore
three princes, yet by
the embalmer's art
outlived them all, hidden
testament to the Book of Rites.

Exhumed from the silken core
of a six-shelled casket
while bamboo musicians kneel
at zithers and clay maidens
poise for a signal,
she preserves the honor
of those who are dust
where the gods of earth
and heaven fail.

# TAKING STOCK

At minus twenty, silence
wears the rough grain
of hills into sun,

everything around here
taut as the angle
between northeast and north.

These days we keep
close to home, our hearts
holed up like animals underground.

Where is the pleasure
of bearing winter
if not in the raw clarity,

sheer glare, or even stillness
that can't be thought?
As far as this place goes

the book of cold,
worth its weight in ignorance,
does for always
what always does for us.

# O'BRIEN'S COVE

On days like this, water breaks
new ground,

giving birth to a hidden place
where the point, bound

by cedar and pine,
is always just beyond

us, taking time
down to its original finish. On

days like this, April
greens the last burrs

of frost from its fur
then stretches across sky until

every reflection cracks
wide open, holding nothing back.

# SWORDSMITH

The Saracens of Damascus
and Spain's Toledo blademakers
approach an intimate truth
of steel and their swords bear
the river's temperament in battle,
yielding at stress, yet keeping
the ravenous edge.
I've only heard this recently
from one who knows their work.
I'm sure, however, none can equal
our ancient mastery for loving
ore into life.
    After fasting, robed in purity,
we dwell with the anvil and consider
the forge whose heart pumps
molten islands through our trust
and we hand-fashion its gift
as sea gods our world before us.
Still, we fold generations
of metal into every blade,
weld and hammer continuously
until air dances with flesh,
then, on the final day, at sunrise
as the white heron fishes
amid its reflection and stones
flower in first light,
we kneel among shadows to pray
before delivering the birth-stroke
from fire to water, Hachiman,
the sword god, seething his praise.

Held upright in a running stream,
an inferior blade may shave
each dead leaf in two
that drifts against its edge,
but ours own the souls of leaves
and all will circle avoiding the touch.
Here, without question, is proof
we are unsurpassed.
I thank you for coming
and pray the gods grant you a son.
As she sleeps,
please lay the sword beside your wife.

## NOVEMBER

It takes shape
as flocks
rising up
stop us cold to watch
their dark bond
with dawn
become grounds
for going, a presence
born again
in every sense
when winds spread
the word
and brown fields bristle like
dense fur
down the back
of the earth.

# THE ILLUMINATION

*for Paul Metcalf* (1917-1999)

As we enter
the old hilltown graveyard,
stone rows rise

toward the church
like a long flight
of stillness, but the afternoon

flows with rain and fog
recalling that Sung Dynasty scroll,
Thatched Hut on Orphan Mountain,

where the nameless hermit
can't be seen.
Just a wild line

of peaks streaming
into clouds
and the blink

of his one room shack
where a candle
is left burning.

# SOLE PURPOSE

*for Julio Granda*

Between how and why,
with a world at stake,
the balance of his nature
fills this studio
where I find him,
brush in hand, waging
war against war,
surrounded by bodies
neither dead nor
dismembered, but vital
and whole, sudden
females swept onto paper,
immense women whose sole
purpose is to make love
tip the scales toward reason,
brash cumulus nudes
exuding life, still wet
from the rush of creation,
covering the walls and floor,
spread across tables and chairs,
over unframed paintings
and paint-scarred easels,
women with no regrets
who burn through grief
until they come
to the hidden core,
all present in flesh and odor,
dampness and heat,
voluptuous, volcanic,
throwing themselves
at the gods of loss
and living to tell about it.

# AUGUST NIGHT, TAOS

Things look up in the wake of rain
as cricket song, rising from sage,
mingles with sudden stars.
Between mountains haunted by
wind and the desert shimmer
of lightning, old powers persist.
We can just make them out, wise
to what never changing is.

When moonlight strikes a cow skull
near the pale adobe wall,
fates like ours rise
above being, but emptiness
holds its ground, the long tradition
we have to fall back on.

# PRINTING IN WINTER

By such work, the eye of a public is attracted, held,
and finally made appreciative, even though the method
by which these results are gained is not realized.
— Daniel Berkeley Updike, *The Black Art: A Homily, 1894*

When the black art calling
leaves me no choice
but to weather the stone
cellar cold, then dead
set on presswork I lock
in the chase, pull
a few proofs, and strip
process down to the bone
joining the primitive sorts
that follow this craft
to the letter, living
an alchemy of ink and lead
with lineage itself
on the line, those stoics
in sync with seclusion,
unobtrusive as details
of their own design,
who make each pressing
need implicit, and whose
lust for what stays
untimely, leaving progress
in the dust, still holds
sway over time,
their black art breed
by the grace
of dissent, going
against the grain.

# NIXON AT YADDO

Awakens at 6 A.M.
to sit lotus-nude on the bed
communing with his muse.
Breathing deeply, a streak
of dream is left in his look
while yesterday's draft lies
on the floor, beginning:
*Let me...*
He peruses the words wistfully
as sunlight crawls
toward him. This room
will witness a distillation
of the McCarthy years
into a moving villanelle.
Crows warp the quiet.
Nixon clucks. Is no place
free from distraction,
from senseless ardor?
He slaps page and pen away,
retrieves them, kneels
at the window
and touches the glass,
the voracious face, the sky's
graying temples.

# SHI HUANG TI
## (d. 210 B.C.)


Interpreting a summer storm
as an act of arrogance,
the First Emperor studied Mt. Xiang
and thought, such derision

cannot go unpunished.
He kept to his tent, reticent
until thunder ebbed,

then emerged to have
three thousand convicts
assembled at once.

The plan? Cut down every tree,
base to summit, and with that accomplished
paint the bare mountain red
as robes of the condemned.

For months he averted his gaze,
but upon completion of the task
walked directly to a nearby clearing
and turned to admire the full effect.

An oriole sang from a hawthorn limb,
southern breeze sweet with pine.

You must be sure to include such details,
he told himself judiciously,
in the arrangement of your afterlife.

# THREAD

You say it was summer,
1948, in the big white
farmhouse, a memory
clear as the footsteps
of your mother and aunt
carrying their dead mother
to the kitchen, when all
that seemed to matter
was a closer look
at the wasted body
naked on the table.
You saw the sewing basket,
bucket, and sponges, but
your mother moved quickly,
grazed your dark hair
with a single kiss and said,
*We should get grandma ready,*
then led you outside
closing the door.
So many years later,
I can see by those words
the way to love,
stitched, like our histories,
into the world.

# CONTINUUM

*The world was a shore, whether sound*
*or form or light, the relic of farewells...*
Wallace Stevens

Storms blacked
the morning out,
but with noon

now floating
some phantom
blues, the lulled

cove tones
everything down.
Honed by horizon,

peaks fall back
into line, and
loons resume

their wary routes
while shadows
leaf through

shallows again.
Open now to
slow reflection,

the limestone
book of changes
claims what

can't be lost.
If returns as is.
Driftwood speaks

for the tribe
that had no word
for wilderness.

# WATER ROUTE

Sailing the inside passage
through late mountain light,
allow for how form and texture
cultivate a mind
roughly like wind and water.
Call each island by the silence
great passion must follow
to teach true perspective.
Let wood rhyme with dolphin,
cloud with salt, north with now,
but consider the course
an ancient scroll
known more for the spirit
of its strict calligraphy
than for the meaning.
Be present as sight
is sworn in by sky and rock
which together make one seam
between desires, between ways to turn.
Get a sharp new take on darkness
and leave arrival
to those who would own
what they can't imagine.
Sailing the inside passage,
watch life eat away at the infinite
until only it remains.

# SUSTENANCE

Tonight I read my daughter
the story of a Cree hunter

who has killed his first birds
in early spring, the Moon of Geese.

He prepares and cooks them himself,
keeping his family silent

during the meal or the bird spirits,
which are stronger than the birds,

might grow angry and change the season's
luck from good to bad.

When all have finished eating,
he collects the bones and sings them

into the fire where they are purified
and returned by way of ashes

to the heart of things: earth and water.
My daughter takes the book she is

too young to read, the wings
of its pages alive in her hands

and wonders what will happen next.
Already, the hunger begins.

# FIRST LESSON
### *(16<sup>th</sup> Century Japan)*

Listen closely:
A cut must echo
in a warrior's mind
even before delivery.
This ample corpse
was a fool dishonored
by careless words,
so while his head
amuses the dogs,
his torso will be your model
for sixteen cutting strokes.
Look, your father's sword
is versed in battle
yet innocent as water
to one whose thirst
consumes him. Such a blade
personifies cause.
Here, let me demonstrate o-kesa,
a cut made obliquely
from shoulder to side.
Notice how talonlike
my hands lock
in agreement with death,
how the shorn limb reflects
style. Much as a lover,
success depends greatly
upon separation
with an eye
toward preserving accord.
It's ironic perhaps,
but view the cut as an image
midway through a poem,

consummating the marriage
of reality and overtone.
And next, to answer
your unasked question,
I shall demonstrate ryo-kuruma,
one plane stroke
through pelvic bone.
Observe my stance,
fluid yet tense,
a completed act
letting time catch up
if you concentrate
on its symmetry and nothing more,
allowing your thoughts to unite
with Buddha
in the absolute light
of the sword.

# THE FINAL TASTE

With bow season almost here,
two whitetail does become moonlight
searching for apples. Down near
the burly old trees they browse like

sisters, or mother and daughter. Quietly
I step out on the porch to get
a better look. Frost arches an ivory
back along midnight. My breath,

given body, tells me I'm destined
for the greatness of fallen apples
going bad on the lawn, this second
discovered by sudden muzzles,

crushed and swallowed, the final taste
of earth putting everything in its place.

# PRAYER

*(Isenfluh, Switzerland)*


Out at daybreak
between white-tiered peaks
and strict tradition,

three generations
haying by hand
know to what lengths

height will go
to wear them down
as they work each shift

of the glacial sun
up against the steepness
with crude wooden rakes

shaping hay into lines
like a physical prayer
which cites

the Old Testament
of soil and rock,
speaks the mind

of wind across centuries,
honors the being
that gives no ground.

# IKEBANA

In the end, knowing hands
with an able mind
make this arrangement
give life that is taken
what is taken for life.
To come up empty and still
find perfect balance
along the way,
bamboo, plum, and pine
work together as new growth.
Through gathered grace,
three opinions rise
above all others from earth
to heaven then slowly back
until nothing appears
symbolic by design
which, in effect,
must always be the point
where past and future
naturally cross,
like one soul landing
while another takes off.

# RELATIVITY IN JANUARY

*Time, space, and matter are interdependent.*

- Einstein, 1916


When the mare cuts loose
across the pasture, her momentum
is the only warmth

drawn from morning, from
a patchwork barn, backdrop pines,
or a wolf moon's fade to blue.

At minus three, after all-night
snow, anything can noun its way
out of motion, but instead

she snorts and bucks, then runs
with the spirit herd deep in her blood.
Tending to hay, I understand

the old rancher who scrawled
an impression of every horse
he ever owned, because that book

alone could move him like gravity
between where and when.
Now, catching wind of an apple,

the mare nickers close.
As she chews, I inch my hands
through her thick winter coat,

edge my face down her neck,
inhaling the dark
incense, amazed at how little

it takes to make the time
of cold, the space of home,
and the matter of bodies connect.

# WHAT WE COME TO

*for Samuel Green*

I'm running late as usual
and the news from everywhere is bad,
but there's your letter on the kitchen table
and I just have to see again
how calligraphy weighs confidence,
how first thing each morning
you track down yesterday's mistakes
in the log addition you're building by hand,
and how much goes into making words
like level and true feel workable as prayer.
Here's that rightness you always dwell on,
the idea of living matter
whose distinction it is to become us
by way of use, so why not celebrate
the cold spring day these trees were felled,
when eagles bred between islands
and fog burned off the sound.
Through your focused lines I can smell
fresh-milled boards of yellow cedar
and strong black coffee on the stove.
I can hear your new wall rise
as you bang in each log dog,
then scribe and cut the notches
until being truly levels with itself.
Love hangs in that balance you call
right work done right, an unsung refrain.
From all there is, hour by hour, it approaches
what we come to.

# ANALEMMA

*A figure-8 formed by recording the sun's position*
*from the same place at the same time of day*
*at regular intervals for a year.*

As if its radiant sound
could make meaning slowly
dawn on me,
I drew the word out
loud through your still life room,
just for the rhythm
at first, but then for that
tone the unknown
sets when knowledge is yet
to come, in this case 9 down
on the crossword
puzzle left beside your bed,
merging a mother's horizon
with the journey of the sun.

# PINE JUDGMENT

### (16th Century Japan)

Straight from battle
before mouths of the dead
go dry or a single
raven appears,
he rides toward the garden
whose silence claims victory
over nothing,
and enters the hut.
Inside, life passes
for a question of steam
curling above tea
until the way is clear.
Even with a world at stake,
he must leave himself
open to the simple matter
of this room
where an heirloom vase
holds one pine branch
bent by centuries
and lichened
to the thought of mist
closing in on distance.

# KINSHIP

On Sundays I work
the dogs in a field
off Route 20: shepherds
bred hard from the oldest German
bloodlines. They foam
and lunge as my eyes
stab into theirs, challenge
on the bowel level never
ignored: they're born loving
gravity. I tell the handlers,
praise each thrust, each seed
of aggression. My thick sleeves,
jute-bound leather, grow
dark as their snarling
jaws and cadent, defiant tails.
With stick hissing, I rile the line
to a prayer of vengeance,
take the bites one by one,
then turn away feigning fear,
submission. Catching my breath
I sense confidence inside them
climb into solitary
devotion. Courage test, ambush,
week after week we define
and redefine the bonds.
Even those Sundays
with rain muzzle-deep
in the marrow of hills
we assemble in this clearing,
resolute, expedient, a solid
pack of animals.

# DRAWING THE LINE

As it stands
only where two things meet
is a true line drawn.
I paper the bedroom
butting patterns to match
what seems plumb, my hope
balancing chance and design
on the point of this job.
Easier to trace
how sharply sky defines hills
on a still day in March,
how caught short between seed
and root, the clock of zero
says bear with me
just a little longer.
While I listen
my daughters drive off,
give a quick wave.
For now, at least, goodbye
implies coming home later.
Back from Guatemala last month,
a friend told of 20 campesinos
killed by soldiers
as they worked the fields,
soldiers we here
don't see in our sleep.
To worry about this
at such distance is a gift
because with the moon no more
than a serif on the elm,
I'll soon be in bed
holding my wife, letting

that warm line between us
run through the night,
across the sky,
and around the world
as many times as it takes
to equal a single hair
on the head
of one murdered worker.

# TRIBAL GATHERING

True to the calling
that calls no
attention to itself,
it starts down
Philbrick Hollow
when a hen pheasant
turns into brush,
her exquisite plainness
ingrained by wild logic,
and before long,
direct yet unassuming
as hands on a loom,
other females arrive
in their hill-blended
yellows, grays,
and browns, wives
mad about purpose
and nourishment,
mothers of low key
beauty, daughters
ordained by earth
to make sense
of tomorrow, women
steeped in secrets
of coyote and lynx,
porcupine and hawk,
with feral vows
passed down
by muskrat and mink,
otter and fox,
a fertile procession,
the subtle presence
of nothing left to chance.

# PACEMAKER

More conscious now
of what keeps time
inside you, I lie awake
and listen to the dark
Atlantic pulse,
our long flock
of years climbing above
the dunes, flying
in the face of change.
A new truth
has led me to this place,
between fear and love,
where I can lose myself
in a heartbeat, where far
from home the music
of how we began
bleeds through moonlight,
wave by wave, memory
breaking on flesh.
Tonight, touch alone
could tide me over,
but as you sleep
our stars shift course
and I drift slowly
past the point
of no return,
pressing close, closer,
feeling your breath
holding my own.

# GARDEN QUILT

Finding beauty in need,
piece by piece,
she plants this garden

giving each bright pattern
the sunlight and rain
of skill and diligence,

art and purpose,
her life like needlework
stemming from hardship

turned into soil,
from the knowledge
that age mulches down

to feed the vision
of a daughter
who will dig and weed

and cultivate her own
fabric of roots,
every stitch

holding its ground,
taut as the seed
her mother had sown.

# CH'I

Embodying
this brush
with it
across white
Sung silk,
ten seconds
centuries old
still quicken
the pulse
of ink through
a few curved
strokes until
the image lives
up to its word,
soundness given
moving grace
as in *horse,*
the character
for, and of.

# MAYFLIES

As an ancient breed
of darkness from the creek
suddenly swirled into long maple light,
they ignore the change
and mate on the wing
filling the sky like revelation
blind to us who seem
no more than soil or wood
or swallows that bolt their pale sealing
of bodies down until this valley
is a sun shower
of sacrifice and desire,
old names we rarely use,
but always answer to.

# DENNIS PORT

At low tide, the sound bares
its soul to scavengers like us,

camping in the ebb of August,
still young, yet old

enough to love
how eons of sand assimilate loss.

We stalk the flats, prodigal
with shells and fiddler crabs,

all blood attuned to the role
of water as our girls

braid kelp into brown tiaras
and gulls skirl over clams.

Now for us, selfish, persistent,
the accent is on back

when you say we've been living
ahead of ourselves,

must find our way
back, urged by tide

as if word and action alone
could impersonate tomorrow.

# THOREAU'S HAT

On a long afternoon walk
pockets run out of room:
stones, acorns, wild fruit,
an arrowhead, a bone.
There must be someplace safe
for one fringed gentian,
a cicada husk,
or an owl feather
still holding the moon.

Five miles to go
before dusk fills the pond,
but there's no hurry.
Nothing comes between
this mind and the world it is
collecting, whose smallest
details are worth
looking into for what
can be made of them.

Back home, with lamplit
harvest before him,
he studies each object closely,
then writes a few words down
while a hornet walks the brim
of his weathered hat,
totally focused, around
and around, until
mystery becomes reason.

# GENETICS

Out here we cross the length of winter
with the breadth of islands to yield
practical words ready for anything,
a strict rhetoric holding water
with traits passed on from maul
and wedge, block and tackle,
from salt-tooled docks in dire straits
and trawlers heaped to the gills
with gear, from livelihoods cut back
in the lean days when tide, fish,
and weather act like gods blessing
hardship, or stories where loss plays
an endless role as it moves us
to repeat what we are made of.

# THE LAWRENCE TREE

On Lobo Mountain, north of Taos, we climb
to the chapel where Lawrence's ashes are mixed
with the concrete of the shrine,
his spirit rising more like the bread he baked
than any sudden phoenix.
Just knowing he split wood, fed
the chickens, and milked the cow
those cool August mornings,
so far from the wars of thought
about him, shines a quiet loneliness
into time unfolding before us.

Here, chores finished, he ate
with Frieda, walked the trails, and wrote
until the long San Cristobal Valley
lay stranded under desert stars.
At the height of summer, we have the place
to ourselves, our low voices
the only sound between his small adobe shack
and the ponderosa pine once painted
by Georgia O'Keeffe, who night after night,
stared up through its branches,
seeing a life against the heavens.

# HOMECOMING

Because it was time to forgive,
one by one, our children came home.
First the eldest, the she-wolf,
light fur bristling,
loped toward the rise of her name.
Then, around noon, a son appeared
in the crown of the dead elm: a flame-
eyed hawk, tempered by distance.
Over the years, karma
had often cracked down
until we learned
to expect nothing, yet slowly,
this day, it led them here.
Windwise, the shy girl, the lynx,
ears erect, stalked unblinking
at her instinct to cover
the lost ground between us.
Now, spared by their return,
we dared not reach out or speak,
but instead kept still as a loss
of memory or desire, alone together,
mated for life, while our youngest,
the green snake,
moved sleeplike through the sun
and onto the porch, purest grace
we had missed much too long.

Next came the eight-point buck,
and snow goose,
and immersed in strength,
the great glistening black bear.
By dusk, as horizon approached
the matter of depth, all had come back
to their birthplace,
where blood could assume a family,
back to bodies before claws
and fur, scales and wings,
to lives we had once conceived
in the way before the war.

# INCENSE

By midnight, the storm clears out unveiling a faint mane of stars
above the ridge. When wind dies down, temperature drops,
and a trailing topline looms into view, lean as November, the whole
galaxy riding on it. From moon-stenciled pines beyond the pasture,
the flooded creek speaks through blackness like blood through muscle
primed for running. Messages on the air, fox scent, deer scent,
mingle with fermented leaves and the memory of rain while back
in the stable horses give off an incense so rich that God, without
a second thought, kneels down to inhale it, the privilege, the loving
that makes wisdom last. Then, sharply as their breathing turns white
and lights the cold, a good killing frost starts to gather in the valley.

after the storm
even moonlight
edgy in its stall

# RIGHT OF WAY

What works best
is the mile walk down Sleepy Hollow
to the tracks, fitting weather
into blood until powers merge
  in a single line.
As for this body of land,
it's on the move, but slow as the story
  of how crows
    include the evening,
one of those friends
whose hair is bound
to change, weight up and down,
mind here and there, no more than that.
   Eyeing hello the ruts, heaves,
crumbling shoulder along the creek,
cornfield giving sky a bearded finish,
  yesterday's footprints,
    pines worth being reborn as
over and over until words
don't have a chance, finally
reach the railroad bridge,
  lean downvalley
where tracks bend west
and after a while that diesel riff
starts to build, full, round, bearlike
through the lowland,
  feel it play the steel
    of the bridge

into arms and legs, louder, triple
locomotives grind a solid clip,
three-minute freight, oilstink, the rock
of boxcars underfoot:
      Boston & Maine, a marsh hawk
rides the updraft, gone,
Western Pacific, Delaware & Hudson,
      back home windows rattling now,
         Potlatch, Cotton Belt,
taste the ultimate rust,
flatcars stacked with lumber,
tankcars mapped by grime,
      Santa Fe, Erie Lackawanna,
         Rio Grande the Action Road,
late news banked off veins of sun,
hoppers of gravel, gray on gray,
      Illinois Central Gulf, Southern
Serves the South, height and depth
coupled by motion, creosote wars
in a broken hand,
      Bangor and Aroostook, Soo Line,
         a shim of distance
fills the gap, Norfolk & Western, B & O,
one world after another,
      Union Pacific, Burlington Northern,
in the long run
so much coming and going
      it doesn't matter why.

# THE ANSWER

All day it snowed,
and now, through stillness
after the storm, coyote howls

clear the midnight hills.
You sit up in bed,
straining to hear each note,

then step softly outside
lofting an answer into the cold.
Weightlessly, your breath dyes

the air white with warmth
northern tribes once called
the blossoming of the stars.

Whatever is echoed
across the deep drifts
will return in secret

later on as I hold you
under the winter quilt,
listening to your heart.

# FOR THE FARM GHOST

Your barn needs work.
The warped boards are diaries of rain,
quietly incoherent,
and more than ever, neglect speaks
for distance, letting termites comb
years out of wood.
All day long, in a living gesture,
it seems to lean slowly toward evening.

Our eyes become lost on the inroads
of the place
as luminous dust veers into breath
and walls read like love
for loss, for the green
of essentials mulched by age.

Around here, as the saying goes, a soul
will follow the grain
and though a century's gone
a caul of silence clings
when I allude to you
in the shattered panes and split beams,
in the foothold of sky
on a dangerous roof.

# RESURRECTION

*To acquire a political meaning*
*you don't even have to be human.*
— Wislawa Szymborska

This far from the capital,
where bloodline tradition still
runs deep, we fan the flames
of your new campaign
through a town square crowd
whose close-knit spirit
and faith-based nature
dovetail so well with our plans.
A homegrown success,
you're in your element
while the gracious mayor,
versed from birth in etiquette,
makes certain you'll be noticed
in the postcard photos
preserving this festive event
along with body part
souvenirs cut from
the accused before the noose
is tightened, unforgiving
judgment that shows
no mercy to the man
found guilty of living.

# LETTERPRESS COMMUNION

*"...in its ultimate analysis the only justification
for human work is an intrinsic sanctity."*
— Eric Gill, *An Essay on Typography*

Here on the beaten path,
what stays the same
makes all the difference.
Trusting in that site
where common ground
is solitude, you are charged
with the hearts of others,
and carry them even farther
than language demands,
convinced their smallest needs
prove measures of connection.
It happens like this:
Something you read becomes
one with you, and with one
hope you ready a berth
from lead, letter by letter,
lines set for life
in three dimensions.
Raised to their highest power,
paper, ink, and typeface
form a trinity you must weigh
as if the past depends on it,
and the past is only now
coming into focus,
like that first love
for presswork, still found
between spirit and process,
upholding the matter of details
keeping the universe honest.

# BEACH TOTEM

On borrowed time, it stands
for all you have left
behind, something nameless

in the name of the washed-up,
the lapsed and forgotten,
remnants joined to give loss,

no matter how tough
or random, another shot
at consequence, roughed out

of driftwood and plastic,
fabric and metal, detailed
with seaweed and egg sac,

feather and shell,
excess rescued from
the depths where passion

has always been raw
material for what doesn't last,
but builds as if it will.

# CONCUBINE

As you dress, early mist
reflects moonlight and silence
between the winter hills

until blackened teeth, shaven
eyebrows, and powdered skin
thrive like secrets on shadow.

That aura caught
by your long brushed hair
is sky whispering

through distance
the old story of youth.
Though you crave your name

on his lips, what if the clock
of hoofs should suddenly
fill the courtyard?

Then who would love
the radiant mist
joining this world to the next?

# THE SALVATION OF HUMOR

When the past broke down
in the wake of her stroke,
my mother couldn't come up
with a single noun for anything,
not a watch, or a pen, or herself, such
small words whose sudden weight
made me see gravity in a whole
new light as if loss played
out like fire, and ninety years began
burning their bridges. For those first
few ER hours, her reply to each
question was more body language
than language, less sound than fury
until, around dawn, a solid word
against the emptiness gained back
an inch of ground. Maybe
syllabic brainwaves clicked,
or a late-breaking drug kicked in,
but it didn't matter. Across that limbo
between lost and found, while
shaky vitals blipped, I finally heard
a coherent response: "Cow," she said,
when asked what she would order
in a restaurant, and her split-screen face
half-laughed along with the rest of us,
so right on cue the young neurologist
smoothed his hand across her blanket
asking, "Now what do you call this,
this thing that keeps you warm?"
Digging deep, gung ho as always
to please, my mother frantically
ransacked the tomb of her memory

and then, almost calm, grasping
some fugitive peace of mind,
she looked at him the way stoics
look at weather, and answered
with embraceable logic,
"I call it," she said, "I call it...
the thing that keeps me warm."

# FOLLOWING THE LIGHT

*Estelí, Nicaragua, July, 1978*

(U.S. financial support kept the brutal Somoza
family regime in power from 1937-1979)

Blind to a husband's anger,
Maria Luz, suburban mother of three,
leaves to attend a meeting of women
who will offer their homes as refuge
for rebels, lend the revolt a hand.
Straight from New England
our money heads south,
but we're planting this garden
before the sun climbs too high.
Alone now, ignoring obstacles
of family and friends that might
slow her down, and with fear the smell
of rotten flesh, burnt plastic and rubber,
she walks streets bristled by markers
naming the dead and disappeared.
A shadow among them,
our money shows up in the form
of guardsmen who steal what they want,
then check her knees and elbows
for cuts or bruises, guerrilla signs.
Allowed to go, she crosses the square
where seven bodies bloat in a stream
of flies, as mouth-covered mourners
claim the blue faces.
True to its roots, our money lies
in wait to break the resistance, but up here,
oblivious, we're done planting,
while each day, risking everything,
she plants her faith in the cause.
Vendors hawk food and the park raves
with sound when she meets a friend
who lost three children in a single year,

whose last daughter still fights in the hills,
who says in a voice like law,
*There is more to life than burying your dead,*
as they walk together through loud waves
of music and people, shadowed
by the money we refuse to see,
out of our hands forever, giving us away.

# LIFE CYCLE

Everything yields when it comes
to this place,
where begin and end begin
to have the same ring
and fields alone make good company.
Echoing a Sung scroll,
early fog inlays the valley
as we bank a wealth of mulch
around shrubs and flowers.

Length times width, our trust
runs clear until odds
are indigenous to love.
The fact is all we own
has always been one up on us
so the pure abundance
of what's left undone
holds a modest world
that much tighter.

Borne by any chore,
the cycle of belonging
must now and then
transcend the past
and who would second guess
the beauty of finding
among lilacs, a daughter's cut hair
swept off the porch last fall
woven through a sparrow's nest.

# VALLEY BLOOD

With sap running early
and a hundred buckets hung,
Leon can barely keep up. While every
maple on the road is tapped, a long

tale of steam joins the sky
to his swayback shed
where I love to sit in the dead
of night, listen, and clear my mind.

He calls childhood a farm
near Greenfield in the Twenties,
and fate his father coming home
one day with news: finally

a decent bull for sale
at a fair price, but before
the man could elaborate, his wife turned pale,
then pointing at the door

said, *you better think real careful
cause if you buy the beast, I'm gone.* Simple
as that. She even twisted her wedding
band off and spent the evening sitting

mute as straw. Leon admits he saw
his father walk to the garden, kneel
down and clench the soil.
Next day he bought

that bull and the wife left. Four
children couldn't stop her.
Leon stares at his half-gnarled,
half-nailed fingers while steam purls

vision and syrup-pans hiss.
He feeds the fire and checks the flow
from pan to pan, a final gold
the embodiment of sweetness.

Then, with an old tin cup, he skims
a taste for both of us, eyes spanned
inward over bluest pain. *No reason
at all,* he declares, *just a fine
Jersey bull, such a beautiful bull, goddamn!*

# LETTERPRESS MEDITATION

"It is the theory of the word for those
for whom the word is the making of the world..."
—Wallace Stevens, *Description Without Place*

About halfway through the run,
with color even and kinks
worked out, rhythm cuts to the chase
as deckled sheets of Rives face
up to rollers, type form, and ink,
their off-white silence broken

by a hand-set black refrain,
hard lines digging in until letters
turn runic, abstract, each page
a pattern light years away
from meaning, but closer than ever
to the world being made.

# AUTUMN CRICKETS

As late sun fades
through the haze
of their sound,
you gently brush
your mother's white hair,
fix her pillows
and clean her glasses
so she can read the paper
then fall asleep.
Outside, fields revive
the sense of ending,
a pulse that grows
fainter every day,
hearts failing like beauty
on the path to itself,
but now you're afraid
because in the perfect
clutter of this farmhouse,
the only thing
there has never been
room for is absence.
Reading the obituaries,
a mystified look
comes over her face,
a sudden confusion when
she can't find her name.
*Didn't you tell anyone?*
With the last round
of crickets drifting off,
you patiently explain

that she isn't dead yet,
then smiling at the strange
and funny sadness of this
unexpected gift, you kiss
her luminous hand.

# TEA GARDEN

Perfectly flawed,
so heart and mind
find nothing beyond being
deep in the mountains,
this garden draws breadth
like a brushstroke.
Open the gate
and take the mapled path.
A thousand miles
fill each step
toward emptiness
until you hold no more
than a weathered scroll
of moss over granite.
Here, the sword passed down
through routes of blood
serves only to cut
a delicate stem, narrow
branch, or bamboo shoot
whose balanced arrangement
illuminates strength.
Before long,
what grows from quiet
gains such beauty in light
of forgetfulness,
the oldest line
of sight comes close enough
to dream, and makes it easy
to see yourself
in the darkened hut,
nameless, high on tea,
gathering all you are.

# ORIGAMI

One last time
hold our children close.
First the older, who will slowly
forget you, and then the baby
who touches your delicate mouth,
each smooth eyefold, and that fragrant
sleep-colored hair.

You must have felt the journey
come to life before we understood
what was happening, an October-like
change in countenance, a pond
abandoned.

But the peaks of your voice
are crystalline with new growth,
acceptance channeling sun into pulse
as our daughters give way
just enough to watch your hands spawn
a swan from paper, deftly,
arced neck and impossible
wings appear.

Inside minutes, complete,
it's set on the mantel
between bronze stag and earthen ram;
suddenly faced
with your leaving,
we cannot fathom the intricacy
of so controlled a flight, your mind
performing as if nourished by loss
for a thousand fragile years.

# YUKON RIVER ORACLE

Just below the Arctic Circle
where current changes
from aspen to wolf
to limestone gray, loon calls

take the shape
of whatever hides longing
in your heart.
Already summer looks frayed

around the edges. Soon
it will break
in the spell
of another season while stars renew

their vows with cold.
Bordering on breath,
a primal rhythm
resonates and slowly grows

until all there is is listening.
It drifts across the distance
to a point
where fate has the ring

of a vast migration. This far north,
the river reflects
everything
life appears to pass for.

# BINARY FISSION

*Reproductive process in which single-celled*
*organisms divide into two new cells, always female.*

Autumn doubles
down on the past,
as my daughters
read these hilltown
graves, sounding out
each granite line
whose hand-carved
name and epitaph
is language squared
with earth and bone.
Nothing I can say
will mean more
than one grave,
recalling my own
first stare, how
the stone cell held

genes for the infinite
tight enough to split.
Path by path,
playing along,
they cross the borders
of centuries,
pox victims here,
lost neighbors there,
a kindred symmetry
reminding me
that the simplest
life will age
to the verge
of death
then blindly divide
into daughters.

# COMING OF AGE

In low sun at the tundra cabin
we feed gray jays by hand.
The kitchen is stocked
and water hauled.
Anything undone can wait.
It's good to see ourselves
as no one else, up here alone,
higher than quiet can say.
Late sky deepens, but light
covers ground, still on the move
past alder and spruce, fragile
muskeg, and staggered peaks.
With blue precision, matter
comes of age in small offerings
which seem to realize life
like a wild mother
who even before she prods
the blind cub to nurse
speaks to it in a secret tongue,
sudden sounds escaping her
unconscious as hope
that we sense around us now
borne back into the earth.

# ACKNOWLEDGMENTS

These poems first appeared in the following publications, sometimes in slightly different versions:

ALASKA QUARTERLY REVIEW: Relativity in January, Thoreau's Hat

APPALACHIA: Yukon River Oracle

ATLANTA REVIEW: Printing by Hand

BELLEVUE LITERARY REVIEW: Autumn Crickets, Thread

BELOIT POETRY JOURNAL: Swordsmith

BIRMINGHAM POETRY REVIEW: Sustenance

COMMONWEAL: Analemma, Beach Totem, Mayflies, Migrations, Quilt

COUNTRY JOURNAL: Taking Stock

THE GETTYSBURG REVIEW: Right of Way

GREEN MOUNTAINS REVIEW: August Night, Taos

JAMA (JOURNAL OF THE AMERICAN MEDICAL ASSOCIATION): The Salvation of Humor

THE LITERARY REVIEW: What We Come To

MID-AMERICAN REVIEW: Binary Fission

THE MIDWEST QUARTERLY: Coming of Age, Drawing the Line, O'Brien's Cove, Tribal Gathering

MINNESOTA REVIEW: Nixon at Yaddo

MODERN HAIKU: Incense

NATURAL BRIDGE: Burning in Spanish

NEW ENGLAND REVIEW: Tea Master

NORTH AMERICAN REVIEW: Ch'i

NOTRE DAME REVIEW: Pacemaker, Sole Purpose

POETRY: First Lesson, Ikebana, Pine Judgment, Tea Garden, Water Route

POETRY EAST: Following the Light, The Answer

POETRY NORTHWEST: For the Farm Ghost, Genetics, Letterpress Communion, Kinship

PRAIRIE SCHOONER: Origami, Shi Huang Ti

QUARTERLY WEST: Honoring the Dust

RIVER STYX: Homecoming

SALAMANDER: Prayer

THE SEWANEE REVIEW: Garden Quilt, The Lawrence Tree, Printing in Winter, Sole Impression

THE SOUTHERN REVIEW: Corcomroe Abbey, Dry Brush Painting of Winter Crows, The Return

SOUTHERN POETRY REVIEW: Life Cycle

SOUTHWEST REVIEW: Dennis Port

TAR RIVER POETRY: The Illumination

VERSE DAILY: Dry Brush Painting of Winter Crows

VIRGINIA QUARTERLY REVIEW: Calligraphy, Concubine

WALLACE STEVENS JOURNAL: Continuum, Letterpress Meditation

WEBER - THE CONTEMPORARY WEST: Godot in Sarajevo, 1993

WILDERNESS: The Final Taste

THE YALE REVIEW: November